For Sara, my best friend.

For Peapack Reformed Church, with
great affection and love.

The Joy of Every Longing Heart:
An Advent Devotional

Alex Arthurs

ISBN: 9798835417292

TABLE OF CONTENTS

INTRODUCTION:

The word Advent is derived from the Latin word *Adventus,* which means arrival. During Advent we remember the first coming of Christ at Christmas and we anticipate the second coming of Christ at the end of time. We remember Christmas—the Word becoming flesh (Jn 1:14); we anticipate our glorious eschatological future—the Lamb coming again to wipe away every tear from our eyes (Rev 21:4). Advent therefore, is a season of memory and expectation; of remembering and longing; of looking back and looking forward, all at the same time.

Our current conception of time is uniquely linear. Everything is always moving forward. Our eyes are glued to the horizon of the future. What's next will inevitably be better than what has already passed. The iPhone 14 is better than the iPhone 1, right? It's just assumed. Frank Sinatra once sang, "The best is yet to come!" We modern-minded folk unflinchingly nod our heads in agreement.

The ancient Hebrews had a vastly different understanding of time. Instead of turning their back on the past and solely looking to the future, as we so often do, one Hebrew scholar explains that the ancient Hebrews *walked backward into the future.*[1] Their eyes were on the past as they backpedaled into what was yet to come. They kept their national history ever

---

[1] This idea of "walking backward into the future" is taken from Travis West, *Biblical Hebrew: An Interactive Approach*, (Wilmore, KY: GlossaHouse, 2016), 68-69.

West writes: "History was not primarily a sequence of events to be placed in correct order. History was represented and celebrated communally through ritual and liturgy. History was the lives and stories of their ancestors which, when remembered and told, ushered them into God's presence. History was sacred. History was sacramental."

before their eyes, even as new chapters unraveled. They were always mindful of the way in which God's gracious intervention punctuated their story even as the clock continued to tick and tock.

During this *Adventus* season, I invite you to "sacramentalize" time in the same way that the ancient Hebrews did. I want you to look back on the past as you walk into God's good future. I want you to relish in God's past salvation story— God coming down to be with us Jesus—even as you anticipate the consummation of our collective salvation— Jesus coming back to make all things new. Advent is all about remembering and anticipating; looking back as you walk forward. My favorite author Frederick Buechner offers us wise counsel:

> The past and the future. Memory and expectation. Remember and hope. Remember and wait. Wait for him whose face we all of us know because somewhere in the past we have faintly seen it, whose life we all of us thirst for because somewhere in the past we have seen it lived, have maybe even had moments of living it ourselves. Remember him who himself remembers us as he promised to remember the thief who died beside him. To have faith is to remember and wait, and to wait in hope is to have what we hope for already begin to come true in us through our hoping. Praise him.[2]

Praise him. It's my deepest longing that by remembering and anticipating, by looking back as you waddle your way into the future, that praise might well up from the deepest depths of your soul. What God has done, He is continuing to do.

---

[2] Frederick Buechner, *Secrets in the Dark: A Life in Sermons*, (New York: Harper Collins, 2006), 64.

What God is continually doing, He will one day bring to completion. Christ has come. Christ's spirit is with us. Christ will come again.

Remember—hope. Remember—wait. Remember— anticipate. Remember—praise Him. This is my Advent invitation to you, dear reader.

It is my heartiest hope that these daily reflections and prayers and weekly poems, hymns, and prompts help you fully enter the remembering and hoping of the Advent season.

The Hope, Peace, Joy, and Love of Christ be with you!

Alex

WEEK 1
HOPE

Defining Hope

Hope (*'hōp*): Desire accompanied by expectation of or belief in fulfillment.[3]

""

And *shall* is the verb of hope. Then death *shall* be no more, neither *shall* there be mourning or crying. Then *shall* my eyes behold him and not as a stranger. Then his Kingdom *shall* come at last and his will *shall* be done in us and through us and for us. Then the trees of the wood *shall* sing for joy as already they sing a little even now sometimes when the wind is in them and underneath their singing, our own hearts too already sing a little sometimes at this holy hope we have.

Frederick Buechner[4]

---

[3] *Merriam-Webster.com Dictionary,* s.v. "hope," accessed August 25, 2022, https://www.merriam-webster.com/dictionary/hope.

[4] Frederick Buechner, *Secrets in the Dark,* 64.

Defining Hope (cont.)

יָחַל) (*ya-khal*): to wait; await.[5]

קָוָה (*qav-ah*): The feeling of tension and expectation as you wait for something.[6]

ἐλπίς (el-pece'): expectation; hope.[7]

*Wait for the LORD; be strong, and let your heart take courage; **wait** for the LORD!*

Psalm 27:14 (NRSV)

*May the God of **hope** fill you with all joy and peace in believing, so that you may abound in **hope** by the power of the Holy Spirit.*

Romans 15:13 (NRSV)

---

[5] *Strong's Bible Concordance*, s.v. "yachal," accessed August 25, 2022, https://www.biblehub.com/hebrew/3176.htm.

[6] The Bible Project, "Hope," YouTube Video, 4:33, Posted by Bible Project, December 7, 2017, https://www.youtube.com/watch?v=4WYNBjJSYvE&t=117s.

[7] *Strong's Bible Concordance*, s.v. "elpis," accessed August 25, 2022, https://www.biblehub.com/greek/1680.htm.

A Poem to Ponder: Hope is The Thing With Feathers

By: Emily Dickinson

"Hope" is the thing with feathers -

That perches in the soul -

And sings the tune without the words -

And never stops - at all -

And sweetest - in the Gale - is heard -

And sore must be the storm -

That could abash the little Bird

That kept so many warm -

I've heard it in the chillest land -

And on the strangest Sea -

Yet - never - in Extremity,

It asked a crumb - of me.[8]

---

[8] Emily Dickinson, "Hope is the thing with feathers", Accessed August 25, 2022, https://poets.org/poem/hope-thing-feathers-254, Public Domain.

A Hymn to Hum: <u>O Come, O Come Immanuel</u>

1 O come, O come, Immanuel,

and ransom captive Israel

that mourns in lonely exile here

until the Son of God appear.

Refrain:

Rejoice! Rejoice! Immanuel

shall come to you, O Israel.

2 O come, O Wisdom from on high,

who ordered all things mightily;

to us the path of knowledge show

and teach us in its ways to go. Refrain

3 O come, O come, great Lord of might,

who to your tribes on Sinai's height

in ancient times did give the law

in cloud and majesty and awe. Refrain

4 O come, O Branch of Jesse's stem,

unto your own and rescue them!

From depths of hell your people save,

and give them victory o'er the grave. Refrain[9]

---

[9] J.M. Neale. *O Come O Come Emmanuel.* 1851, Source: https://hymnary.org/text/o_come_o_come_emmanuel_and_ransom, Public Domain.

A Question to Consider

In a world fraught with darkness,

saturated in pain,

filled with confusion,

and dripping with despair…

<u>Do you dare hope?</u>

A Place to Pray

Take this space to journal a prayer or two.

_____

_____

_____

_____

_____

_____

_____

_____

_____

_____

_____

_____

_____

_____

_____

The First Sunday in Advent: Hope Sunday

But we have this hope as an anchor for the soul, firm and secure.

Hebrews 6:19a

In the classic movie *Shawshank Redemption,* the protagonist, a freshly imprisoned inmate named Andy Dufresne is conversing with a long-time prisoner of the Shawshank State Prison named Red. Red, a seasoned jailbird, seeking to instill the bleak, sobering, and hopeless reality of imprisonment in the new inmate's soul, says to Andy, "Let me tell you something, my friend. Hope is a dangerous thing. Hope can drive a man insane." Optimistic Andy, not yet scarred by and assimilated to the dreadful life behind bars, replies, "Remember Red, hope is a good thing, maybe the best of things, and no good thing ever dies."[10]

Hope is dangerous; hope is good. Hope can drive a man insane; hope is the best of all things. Hope never dies. Advent is a season of hope. Hope is equal parts memory and expectation; one part remembering, one part anticipating. During Advent, we look back on all that God has done, and we look forward, knowing what He has done, He continues to do, and what He continues to do, He will one day bring to a consummate end—an end where there is no more death, no more tears, no more mourning, and no more pain (Rev 21:4), an end where God Himself will be our light and the Lamb will be our lamp (Rev 22:5), an end where we will drink of the Water of Life and eat of the fruit of the Tree of Life (Rev

---

[10] Frank Darabont, *Shawshank Redemption,* directed by Frank Darabont, written by Stephen King, (1994; Los Angeles: Warner Brothers, 2005), DVD.

22:14)—an end that is "immeasurably far better than anything we could ask or imagine" (Eph 3:21).

What hope! This Advent, will you allow this high and holy hope to anchor your soul?

Prayer: *God of hope, You came to us once in the person of Jesus. You promise to come to us again. Help me hold onto this hope as an anchor for my soul. Amen.*

The First Monday in Advent

Therefore, the Lord himself will give you a sign: See, the virgin will conceive, have a son, and name him Immanuel.

Isaiah 7:14

South African Archbishop Desmond Tutu once recounted the story of a Jewish man in a concentration camp who had been forced to clean the despicable camp toilets. The man knelt with his hands immersed, swabbing and scrubbing away at the unspeakable filth. As the poor prisoner swabbed and scrubbed, his Nazi overseer sought to further humiliate him. "Where is your God now?" the guard sneered. "Where is your God now?" Quietly, without removing his hands from the toilet, the prisoner replied, "My God is right here with me...in the muck."[11]

The baby soon to be born in Bethlehem is Immanuel—"God with us". Not "God removed from our experience". Not "God looking down from a distance". Not "God who doesn't dare get his hands dirty". No, the baby being carried in Mary's womb is Immanuel—God *with* us. In Jesus, God comes as close to us as He possibly can. In Jesus, God fully understands our human experience. In Jesus, God fully comprehends our finite human intricacies and complexities. In Jesus, God hungers and thirsts. In Jesus, God endures trial and temptation. In Jesus, God rejoices and grieves. In Jesus, God cries and laughs. In Jesus, God grapples pain and even death. In Jesus, God fully understands the messiness, the human-ness, of our humanity.

---

[11] Pete Greig, *God on Mute: Engaging the Silence of Unanswered Prayer,* (Grand Rapids: Zondervan, 2020), 191.

On this first Monday of Advent, rest assured that the God who took on flesh by being birthed in a backwater town, in an off-the-beaten-path manger, among slop troughs and hay bales is with you, even, and especially, "in the muck".

Prayer: *Incarnate God, I name some "muck" I'm currently wading through. Come close to me. Walk with me through it. Amen.*

The First Tuesday in Advent

The people walking in darkness have seen a great light; a light has dawned on those living in the land of darkness.

Isaiah 9:2

During my senior year at Hope College, I took a class entitled Positive Psychology taught by the wise Dr. Charlotte vanOyen-Witvliet. Positive Psych was not a happy-clappy, "just think positive thoughts", "manifest your best intentions" kind of class. No. This was a class about cultivating hope in despair, forgiveness amid betrayal, and light in the darkest recesses of the human psyche.

One class period captured the essence of this class most poignantly. Dr. Witvliet asked one of her friends, the talented Carol Roeda, to join us. Carol Roeda introduced herself as an artist and explained that we were all going to take part in one of her favorite artistic exercises: we were going to color out the darkness. Carol began by reading us this very passage from Isaiah: "The people walking in darkness have seen a great light; a light has dawned on those living in the land of darkness." She then told us a particularly painful piece of her own story.[12] After enduring this episode of profound pain, she said, "All felt dark. I felt broken. Dirty. Beyond repair. I was lost in darkness." She went on, "But art was healing. Through artistic expression, God empowered me, quite literally, to color out the darkness." After vulnerably sharing with us, Carol handed out black pieces of paper and white crayons. She succinctly instructed us, "Color out the darkness—in whatever way feels most fitting."

---

[12] To honor the sacredness of Carol's story, I won't repeat it here.

Not having an artistic bone in my body, I scribbled my black piece of paper like a kindergartner until it was Crayola white. And as I did, I felt the strangest sensation. An unknown, previously unnamed weight suddenly lifted. My shoulders untensed. My neck loosened. My heart soared. The exercise was therapeutic, healing, freeing...prophetic. The passage she read at the beginning of the exercise grew lungs and limbs and came to life, "The people walking in darkness have seen a great light; a light has dawned on those living in the land of darkness." I saw a light I didn't know I needed to see.

There's a lot of darkness in our world and our rods and cones too easily adjust to it. In the dark, we carry around burdens we don't need to carry. In the dark, we lose sense of who we are and what we were made to do. In the dark, we stumble into identities that are false and suffocating. The more time we spend in the dark, the more normal the oppressive darkness feels.

The good news of this season is that though the darkness is subtle and enveloping, the light of Christ shines in it and through it. And no darkness can overcome our perfect Luminary.

Prayer: *Light of the World, I name all that feels dark, depressing, and desolate in my life and in the world. Shine in me anew. May your light of love reign supreme in my heart and soul. Amen.*

The First Wednesday in Advent

Then a shoot will grow from the stump of Jesse, and a branch from his roots will bear fruit.

Isaiah 11:1

In May of 2019, I had just finished seminary, my wife, Sara, had just finished her 3rd year of teaching, and we were about to move from Michigan to New Jersey. With all the present excitement and future change on the horizon, we decided that we needed to take a vacation. So we went to Jamaica! And it was spectacular, *'mon*! The beaches were pristine, the greenery was lush, and the tropical air was hot, humid, and heavy. It was paradise; exactly what we both needed. But, upon returning to Michigan, what we both missed most about Jamaica was not the beaches, the tropical weather, or even the rum…we missed *the fruit!* Back in Michigan, we longed for the fresh papaya, ripe pineapple, sweet and spicy mango, and golden bananas we had enjoyed in Caribbean paradise. The fresh Jamaican fruit was the *pièce de résistance* of our tropical getaway.

We're tempted to think that King David is the branch from the stump of Jesse who will "bear fruit" since David was Jesse's son. Don't get me wrong, King David did many admirable and righteous deeds. He was even called, "a man after God's own heart" (1 Sam 13:14). Though David sure had a very light bright side, he, too, had a dark and dangerous shadow side. "The man after God's own heart" was also extremely insecure, calculatingly deceptive, and greedily self-interested.

Overtaken by his shadow side, "the man after God's own heart" committed adultery with his best friend's wife, had his best friend killed, and then tried to cover the whole thing up (2 Sam 11). Is King David really the shoot from the stump of Jesse who bore the promised messianic fruit?

During Advent, we acknowledge that the coming Christ child is the king from the lineage of Jesse, that David was supposed to be. Whereas David's fruit tastes mixed at best, Jesus' fruit tastes like choice bread and fine wine—like our lavish salvation.

Prayer: *Bread of Life, feed my faith. Pour Your Spirit out on me anew today. May I ingest your love so that I might be Your loving presence to my neighbor. Amen.*

The First Thursday in Advent

Righteousness will be a belt around his hips; faithfulness will be a belt around his waist.

Isaiah 11:5

I was nervous. My armpits were sweaty, my face was flushed, my jaw was tight, and my gut was knotted. It was my first meeting as a Commissioner on the Commission on History for the Reformed Church in America, and I already felt totally out of my depths. Just about everyone in the room had a Ph.D. or was working on a Ph.D. and I was still working on my master's degree! On top of that, all the men on the Commission were wearing bowties. I glanced down at the naked collar of my button-down dress shirt. Clearly, I had not gotten the memo. My now friend and mentor, Steve Pierce, the moderator of the Commission said, "Alex, our first order of business is to get you a bowtie. Male Commissioners must wear bowties."

Clothes tell us a lot about a person. Businessmen and businesswomen wear suits. Police officers wear blue uniforms and badges. Judges wear robes. Male History Commissioners wear bowties!

The Prophet Isaiah tells us a little bit about Jesus' wardrobe. He says Jesus will wear two belts—a belt of righteousness— meaning he will embody a true, perfect, and pure humanity; and a belt of faithfulness— meaning He will never give up on us.

As we gaze upon Jesus' appearance, we see the purest form of goodness and we see the loyalist of friends. We see spotless holiness and a companion who will never abandon us. We see the blameless Passover Lamb who takes away the sin of the whole world and our greatest ally who will never leave us nor forsake us. Indeed, clothes tell us a lot about a person.

Prayer: *Righteous and Faithful God, I thank you that through faith I am "clothed with Christ". Today, help me embrace my identity as a new creation in Your Beloved Son. Amen.*

The First Friday in Advent

A voice of one crying out: Prepare the way of the Lord in the wilderness; make a straight highway for our God in the desert.

Isaiah 40:3

After calling New Jersey home for 6 months, Sara and I road-tripped back to West Michigan for Christmas. We left right after the candlelight Christmas Eve service and drove straight through the night. We spent hours on I-80, winding through New Jersey, Pennsylvania, and Ohio. After 4 or so hours on the Ohio Turnpike, the sun slowly began to peek its head above the horizon, and as it did, we passed a deep blue sign that read, "Welcome to Pure Michigan". No sooner than we saw the sign, did we feel our Volkswagen Jetta bump and bang over our home state's cratered roads. For 6 months we had gotten used to the smooth New Jersey freeways. Quickly, we had to get re-acquainted with the pothole-littered highways of the Great Lake State.

As you prepare to welcome Jesus this Advent, do you have any potholes in your heart? Is the terrain of your heart rough with resentment or broken with bitterness? Might you be walking around with an open wound that desperately needs to be mended and bandaged? There's an old saying goes, "Hurt people hurt people." Might you be unintentionally and unconsciously transmitting hurt that needs to be healed?

I love these words from the classic Christmas Carol, *O Little Town of Bethlehem:* "Cast out our sin and enter in. Be born in us today." Be born in us today. What needs to be confessed, healed, and mended so that Christ might be born in you this Christmas?

Prayer: *Healing God, I lay my life's potholes at your feet. Balm and mend my wounded heart, smooth out the rough terrain of my soul, excavate, reconstruct, and restore in the way only You can. Amen.*

The First Saturday in Advent

The glory of the Lord will appear, and all humanity together will see it,
for the mouth of the Lord has spoken.

Isaiah 40:5

I got a call on a sunny Friday afternoon in October from Dan's girlfriend. She said he had been admitted to the hospital in Hackettstown. I rushed up Route 206 in my white Nissan Juke to give Dan[13] a visit. It was a short visit. He didn't look well and he could barely speak. I read him Psalm 23, prayed for him, and left him to rest. I told Dan I'd be back to visit him on Tuesday with Communion.

Tuesday came and I called Dan's girlfriend to confirm that he was still in the hospital, and I learned, to my great surprise, that he was now at home in hospice care. His girlfriend informed me that his condition was deteriorating rapidly and he may be living out his final hours. So, I gathered a loaf of bread and some grape juice and sped along the winding roads and rolling hills to Dan's house. When I entered through his front door, commotion and chaos was palpable. I could hear heart-beat monitors beeping and the feet of nurses thumping all about the house. As I took off my shoes, one of the nurses rushed toward me and blurted out of breath through hefty gasps, "His heartbeat is ever-so-faint. You better hurry, Pastor."

I entered Dan's bedroom. Dan was laying on his side. His face was gray. His girlfriend was holding his hand. Her face was red. Make-up was running down her cheeks in clumpy

---

[13] "Dan" was not this man's real name. His name has been changed for the sake of privacy and respect.

black streaks. A holy heaviness settled upon me as I gripped the magnitude of the moment. I broke the bread: The Body of Christ, given for you. I put no more than a crumb in Dan's mouth. He labored to chew. I poured out the cup: The Blood of Christ shed for you. I guided no more than a drop of grape juice into Dan's mouth. He labored greatly to swallow. I prayed over Dan one last time: "The Lord bless you and keep you. The Lord make his face shine upon you and be gracious to you. The Lord lift his countenance upon you and give you His peace." And as I muttered that blessing with my heart in my throat, a peace settled over the room that I can only liken to the glory and presence of God, and all of us—Dan, Dan's girlfriend, the nurses, my Elder sidekick and I—we saw it together. The mouth of the Lord had spoken.

Jesus was just as present in the bread, cup, and blessing that day in Dan's bedroom as he was in the manger that first Christmas morning. Thanks be to God that He reveals His glory to us in real, feelable, tangible ways. May we have eyes to see it.

Prayer: *God of trumpet blasts and still small silence, tune my ear to hear Your voice and adjust my eyes to behold Your ever-present glory. Instill in me a sense of wonder. Amen.*

WEEK 2

PEACE

Defining Peace

Peace (*ˈpēs*): A state of tranquility or quiet.[14]

""

True peace is not merely the absence of tension; it is the presence of justice.

Martin Luther King Jr[15]

""

Jesus, properly understood as *shalom* (peace), coming into the world from the *shalom* (peaceable) community of the Trinity, is the intention of God's once-and-for-all mission. That is, the mission of birthing and restoring *shalom* (peace) to the world is in Christ, by Christ, and for the honor of Christ.

Randy Woodley[16]

---

[14] Merriam-Webster.com Dictionary, s.v. "peace," accessed August 25, 2022, https://www.merriam-webster.com/dictionary/peace.

[15] Martin Luther King Jr, *A Martin Luther King Treasury*, (Yonkers: Educational Heritage, 1964), 30.

Defining Peace (cont.)

שָׁלוֹם (*sha-lom*): completeness, soundness, welfare, peace.[17]

εἰρήνη (*eye-rain-ay*): One, peace, quietness, rest.[18]

May the Lord give strength to His people! May the Lord bless His people with **peace!**

Psalm 29:11 (NRSV)

Peace *I leave with you; my* **peace** *I give to you. I do not give as the world gives. Do not let your hearts be troubled, and do not let them be afraid.*

John 14:27 (NRSV)

---

[16] Randy Woodley, *Shalom and the Community of Creation: An Indigenous Vision*, (Grand Rapids: Eerdmans, 2012), 25.

[17] *Strong's Bible Concordance*, s.v. "shalom," accessed August 25, 2022, https://biblehub.com/hebrew/7965.htm.

[18] *Strong's Bible Concordance*, s.v. "eirene," accessed August 25, 2022, https://biblehub.com/greek/1515.htm.

A Poem to Ponder

The Peace of Wild Things
By: Wendell Berry

When despair for the world grows in me

and I wake in the night at the least sound

in fear of what my life and my children's lives may be,

I go and lie down where the wood drake

rests in his beauty on the water, and the great heron feeds.

I come into the peace of wild things

who do not tax their lives with forethought

of grief. I come into the presence of still water.

And I feel above me the day-blind stars

waiting with their light. For a time

I rest in the grace of the world, and am free.[19]

---

[19] Wendell Berry, *The Peace of Wild Things and Other Poems,* (New York City: Penguin Random House, 2018).

Hymn to Hum: <u>Let All Mortal Flesh Keep Silence</u>

1 Let all mortal flesh keep silence
and with fear and trembling stand;
ponder nothing earthly-minded,
for with blessing in his hand
Christ, our God, to earth descending,
comes our homage to command.

2 King of kings, yet born of Mary,
as of old on earth he stood,
Lord of lords in human likeness,
in the body and the blood
he will give to all the faithful
his own self for heav'nly food.

3 Rank on rank the host of heaven
spreads its vanguard on the way
as the Light from Light, descending
from the realms of endless day,
comes the pow'rs of hell to vanquish
as the darkness clears away.

4 At his feet the six-winged seraph,
cherubim with sleepless eye,
veil their faces to the presence
as with ceaseless voice they cry:
"Alleluia, alleluia!
Alleluia, Lord Most High!"[20]

---

[20] Gerard Moultry, *Let All Mortal Flesh Keep Silence* 1864, Source: https://hymnary.org/text/let_all_mortal_flesh_keep_silence, Public Domain.

A Question to Consider

With holiday get-togethers piling up,

and presents that still need to be bought,

and end of the year details that need tidying,

with your mind swirling,

and your shoulders aching,

and your neck tightening…

<u>Might God be offering you His peace?</u>

A Place to Pray

Take this space to journal a prayer or two.

_____

_____

_____

_____

_____

_____

_____

_____

_____

_____

_____

_____

_____

The Second Sunday in Advent: Peace Sunday

For a child will be born for us, a son will be given to us, and the government will be on his shoulders. He will be named Wonderful Counselor, Mighty God, Eternal Father, Prince of Peace.

Isaiah 9:6

One of my favorite Christmas carols is *O Holy Night*. It goes like this (sing along if you know it!):

O Holy Night; the stars are brightly shining;

it is the night of our dear Savior's birth.

Long lay the world in sin and error pining;

'til He appeared and the soul felt its worth.

A thrill of hope a weary world rejoices,

'til yonder breaks a new and glorious morn.

Fall on your knees!

O hear the Angel voices, "O night divine!"

Truly He taught us to love one another;

His law is love and His gospel is peace.

Chains shall He break, for the slave is our brother;

And in His name, all oppression shall cease.

Sweet hymns of joy in grateful chorus raise we;

Let all within us praise His holy name!

Fall on your knees!

O hear the Angel voices, "O night divine! [21]

Jesus is the Prince of Peace. At his coming breaks "a new and glorious morn" in which all chains will be broken, and all oppression will cease.

The peace Jesus brings is deeply disruptive and extraordinarily costly. Christ does not come to bless the status quo, He comes to turn over the tables of sin, oppression, and injustice so that the entire created order might flourish—disruptive. The peace Jesus establishes is only possible by Him laying down His very life: "For He himself is our peace and has destroyed the barrier, the dividing wall of hostility through the cross" (Eph 2:14, 16). His dire fate is foreshadowed at His birth when one of the wisemen offers Him the gift of myrrh, an embalming oil— costly.

What do you make of Jesus' disruptive and costly peace? Will you allow your life to be disrupted by Him? Will you allow your heart to be moved by His costly fate?

Prayer: *God of justice and peace, I admit I'm reluctant to accept necessary disruptions that bring about Your peace. I, too, am slow to recognize the price You paid to establish Your peace. Create in me a heart that is receptive to Your disruptive and costly Divine peace. Amen.*

---

[21] John S Dwight and Placide Clappeu, *Oh, Holy Night,* 1847, Source: https://hymnary.org/text/o_holy_night_the_stars_are_brightly_shin, Public Domain.

The Second Monday in Advent

Then the angel told her: "Do not be afraid, Mary, for you have found favor with God."

Luke 1:30

The command: "Do not be afraid" appears three hundred sixty-five times in the Bible. Though the Old and New Testaments were written long before the invention of our modern 12-month, 365-day calendar, this coincidence is quite curious. "Coincidences are God's way of staying anonymous," my Old Testament professor Dr. Carol Bechtel would tell our class. Perhaps this coincidence has God's fingerprints all over it.

We humans are anxious by nature. We are hardwired to be on edge. For a great while the survival of our species depended on it. This instinctual anxiety kept us sheltered, watered, and fed. And yet time and time again, Scripture commands us: "Do not be afraid".

Do not be afraid. Easier said than done. How are we supposed to *just stop* being afraid? Are we to internally say, "No!" every time a worried thought enters our headspace? Are we to ignore our gut when it trembles with uneasiness? Are we to block out, repress, and disregard any inkling of fear before it settles into our consciousness and makes its home in our neck and shoulders? How do we faithfully adhere to this oft-repeated command?

Maybe "Do not be afraid" is less about avoiding feeling scared and more about trusting God amid feeling scared. Maybe "Do not be afraid" is an invitation to see that the fear-invoking predicament, place, or person pales in comparison to the fiery fierce faithfulness of our loving God. Maybe "Do not be afraid" is less about stopping up our ears so that the fear "can't get in" and more about falling backward into God's goodness when we find our heads spinning and our hearts overwhelmed. Frederick Buechner once wrote, "The grace of God means something like: Here is the world. Beautiful and terrible things will happen. Do not be afraid. I am with you. Nothing can ever separate us. It's for you I created the universe. I love you."[22]

Do not be afraid. Trust God. He loves you.

Prayer: *Gracious God, I take off and set down the worries I've been unnecessarily carrying around for days, weeks, months, years, and even, decades. I cast all my anxieties on you because you care for me and love me (1 Pet 5:7). Amen.*

---

[22] Frederick Buechner, *Wishful Thinking: A Seeker's ABC*, (New York: Harper Collins, 1993), 39.

The Second Tuesday in Advent

"Now listen: You will conceive and give birth to a son, and you will name him Jesus."

Luke 1:31

"Liv and Isla!" Sara exclaimed, "How beautiful!" We were on our gray living room couch FaceTiming with Sara's brother, Michael, and my sister-in-law, Audrey. They had just told us the names of their twin girls, our nieces, who were 2 weeks away from delivery. Since that call, Liv and Isla have happily and healthily entered the world. We got to hold both of them while we were back in Michigan this past summer!

In the ancient world, your name encapsulated your identity, vocation, and destiny. The name that is translated "Jesus" in English is the Hebrew name *"Yeshua"*, which means "God saves". Surprisingly, this is not the first time the name *Yeshua* appears in the Bible. Joshua, the Old Testament successor of Moses, was also named *Yeshua*. Both *Yeshuas,* Joshua and Jesus, fully embodied their name, but in vastly different ways. Joshua saved the people of God by way of military leadership and force, leading Israel into the promised land. Jesus saved God's people by taking on the limitations of human flesh, living a faultlessly obedient life, going the way of the cross, and rising from the dead. I wonder what Mary thought of her child's name. I wonder if she thought the child in her womb would save the people of God by personifying the first *Yeshua's* military might, or if she had an inkling that her *Yeshua* would save the people of God by offering Himself as a suffering sacrificial servant.

Prayer: *Jesus, how beautiful is Your name! Let me never forget the power of Your name: You alone can save. Amen.*

The Second Wednesday in Advent

"For nothing will be impossible with God."

Luke 1:37

Headlights shone across our living room TV screen that had George Bailey's big bright face on it. It was Christmas Eve, we were watching *It's A Wonderful Life*, and our long-awaited guests were finally here! Grandma and Grandpa had arrived! My brother Patrick and I put on our coats, hats, mittens, and boots and inhaled the delectable smells of browning steak and garlicky potatoes as we passed through the kitchen and went outside to welcome them.

"Merry Christmas, kids!" My grandpa bellowed deeply as if he were St. Nick himself. He asked if I could give him a hand with the presents, so I took the big bundle and headed for the front door, while Patrick walked my grandma in through the garage. I discarded my boots and set the presents on the bright red tree skirt that sat underneath our six-foot fake tree that was adorned with red and green balls and homemade ornaments. I was admiring a clumsily cut paper snowman ornament I made in the third grade when I heard a massive commotion in the garage. I hurried off to the garage and saw my grandma on the ground. She had fallen. Her foot looked crooked. "I think I broke it," she said in a pained whisper.

The broken foot on Christmas Eve ended up catalyzing the end of her life. A week after her broken foot, she decided to stop her dialysis treatments. She was put into hospice care. After a week in hospice care, she passed away. For that two-week span, as I witnessed her slowly fading away, I prayed that God would heal her, "For nothing is impossible with God," I thought. But my innocent prayers went unanswered.

What do we do with this line from the Angel? We can't help but wonder why God doesn't answer our most desperate pleas and helpless prayers.[23] For nothing is impossible with God...right?

Perhaps it's important to remember here that just because God doesn't answer all our prayers, doesn't mean that he doesn't answer any. God does answer prayer. If you don't believe me, journal your prayers and then keep track. God answers prayer. Truly, nothing is impossible for God—the Creator, Sustainer, and Redeemer of the cosmos—the One whom death could not hold.

God proves He is a God of possible impossibilities by setting His salvation story into motion through an unseemly virgin— an unmarried, impoverished, highschooler will bear the King of Kings and Lord of Lords. Surely, nothing is impossible with God.

Prayer: *Faithful God, I admit that I harbor a bit of resentment toward You for not answering some of my prayers in the way I would have liked. I may not understand why You don't answer all my prayers, but, in Jesus, I see Your steadfast heart and I choose to trust You even when I don't understand. Amen.*

---

[23] For an excellent resource on unanswered prayer, I'd highly recommend Pete Greig's *God on Mute: Engaging the Silence of Unanswered Prayer,* Grand Rapids: Zondervan, 2020.

The Second Thursday in Advent

And Mary said, "Here I am, the servant of the Lord. Let it be with me according to Your will."

Luke 1:38

In the introductory scene of J.R.R. Tolkien's classic, *The Hobbit*, Gandalf the Gray, one of the five wizards in Middle Earth, knocks on Bilbo Baggins' circular door. Bilbo is a hobbit. Hobbits are halfling homebodies who love to eat, drink, and be merry. Gandalf says to Bilbo, "I am looking for someone to share in an adventure that I am arranging, and it's very difficult to find anyone." Bilbo scoffs, "I should think so—in these parts! We are plain quiet folk who have no use for adventures. Nasty disturbing uncomfortable things! Adventures make you late for dinner!"[24]

Like Bilbo, reluctance, uneasiness, and skepticism probably filled Mary's heart and settled heavily into her gut when the Angel appeared in her bedroom and informed her that she was going to give birth to the redeemer of the world. Yet, Mary perceives God speaking an emphatic, "Yes!" to her, so she, in return, speaks an emphatic, "Yes!" back to God: "Here I am," she says, "the servant of the Lord. Let it be with me according to Your will."

God has already said "Yes!" to you in Jesus. In Christ, you are predestined, called, justified, and glorified (Rom 8:30). In light of God speaking an emphatic "Yes!" to you, how might you say "Yes!" back to God today?

---

[24] J. R. R Tolkien, *The Hobbit Or There and Back Again*, (New York: Ballantine, 1996), 4.

Might God be asking you to take a step of faith into an uncomfortable conversation you've been avoiding? Might God be asking you to forgive an enemy you have long harbored a grudge against? Might God be asking you to pray for a person at work you don't know too well? Might God be calling you into an unknown adventure...even if it makes you a couple of minutes late for dinner?

Prayer: *God of Love, I love because You first loved me. I can choose You, only because You've first chosen me. Strengthen my faith to choose Your narrow way that leads to abundant life today. Amen.*

The Second Friday in Advent

Then Elizabeth exclaimed with a loud cry: "Blessed are you among women, and your child will be blessed!"

Luke 1:42

It was approaching dusk. We were trekking up the back of an Everest-esque dune. Mosquitos were buzzing in and out of our ears. Our shirts were damp with sweat and stuck to our backs. Our cheeks were sun-kissed from a day in the sun. "Why are we doing this?" Sara asked as she used both of her hands to swat away a stubborn 'skeeter swarm. "Just trust me, it will be worth it," I reassured her, though I was not anticipating the sweltering sweatiness nor the maddening mosquitos.

When we finally reached the summit of the dune, the sun was just below the Lake Michigan waterline. Deep purples and blazing oranges painted the sky. The waves gently crashed ashore one after the other. We took in the peaceful serenity. Then I pulled out the ring, got down on my knee, and asked Sara *the* question, "Will you marry me?" "Are you serious!?" She repeated again and again. "Yes! Of course, I will!" My heart eased and my soul jumped for joy. "I have another surprise," I smirked. With joy leaking from our eyes and streaming down our faces, we stumbled down the steep dune toward the shoreline, and there, tucked around the corner of the dune, at the edge of the water, were our best friends with freshly popped bottles of champagne.

When something joyous happens, the first thing we want to do is share our joy with others. Upon learning that she will bear and birth Jesus, Mary runs to her relative Elizabeth and shares the news with her, and her joy multiplies. That's the thing about joy; the more of it we share with others, the more of it we feel. Joy is exponentially multiplicative.

Prayer: *Triune God, Father, Son, and Holy Spirit, the prophet Zephaniah says, "You rejoice over us with singing" (Zeph 3:17). Tune my ears to hear your lovely voice rejoicing over me today. Amen.*

The Second Saturday in Advent

And Mary said, "My soul magnifies the Lord, and my spirit rejoices in God my Savior because he has looked with favor on the humble condition of his servant."

Luke 1:46-48

What does it mean to be humble? When a boisterous, arrogant, narcissistic public figure announces their greatness for the millionth time, we say, "Boy, he or she needs a slice of humble pie." When we urge and elbow our child or grandchild to share with a friend or relative that they got an "A" on their history project, but their lips stay locked and their cheeks turn red, we say, "Oh, quit being so humble!" Is humbleness, simply, not being a loudmouth know-it-all? Is humbleness, simply, not sharing our accolades, even though we earned them? What does it mean to be humble?

The author of the book of Numbers wrote, "Now Moses was a very humble man, more humble than anyone else on the face of the earth" (Num 9:12). Do you know who wrote the book of Numbers? Moses! How did Moses exemplify his holy humbleness? Moses was humble because he understood himself. In the Exodus story, Moses knew he had a speech impediment, so he asked God if his brother, Aaron, could speak on his behalf to the nation of Israel (Ex 6:30-7:1). Humbleness is not dishonest self-deprecation, but honest self-awareness. God chose Mary to carry and birth His Son, not because she was lowly, bashful, and timid, but because *God knew that Mary knew that* she was capable of being the *Theotokos*—the bearer of God.

Prayer: *Humble Jesus, teach me true humility. Show me who I really am, and in Your grace, help me to embrace my gifts and limitations. Amen.*

WEEK 3

JOY

Defining Joy

Joy (*'joi*): *the emotion evoked by well-being, success, or good fortune or by the prospect of possessing what one desires.*[25]

""

We never take credit for our moments of joy because we know that they are not man-made and that we are never really responsible for them. They come when they come. They are always sudden and quick and unrepeatable. The unspeakable joy sometimes of just being alive. The miracle sometimes of being just who we are with the blue sky and the green grass, the faces of our friends and the waves of the ocean, being just what they are. The joy of release, of being suddenly well when before we were sick, of being forgiven when before we were ashamed and afraid, of finding ourselves loved when we were lost and alone. Joy is a mystery because it can happen anywhere, anytime, even under the most unpromising circumstances, even in the midst of suffering, with tears in its eyes. Even nailed to a tree.

Frederick Buechner[26]

---

[25] *Merriam-Webster.com Dictionary*, s.v. "joy," accessed August 25, 2022, https://www.merriam-webster.com/dictionary/joy.

[26] Frederick Buechner, *The Hungering Dark,* (New York: Seabury Press, 1968), 102.

Defining Joy (cont.)

שִׂמְחָה (*smi-chah*): joy, gladness, mirth.[27]

Χαρά (*chara*): Joy, gladness, a source of joy.[28]

Do not grieve, for the **joy** *of the Lord is your strength.*
Nehemiah 8:10 (NRSV)

Rejoice *in the Lord always; I say it again,* **Rejoice***!*
Philippians 4:4 (NRSV)

---

[27] *Strong's Bible Concordance*, s.v. "smichah," accessed August 26, 2022, https://biblehub.com/hebrew/8057.htm.

[28] *Strong's Bible Concordance*, s.v. "chara," accessed August 26, 2022, https://biblehub.com/greek/5479.htm

A Poem to Ponder: <u>Don't Hesitate</u>

By: Mary Oliver

If you suddenly and unexpectedly feel joy,

don't hesitate. Give in to it. There are plenty

of lives and whole towns destroyed or about

to be. We are not wise, and not very often

kind. And much can never be redeemed.

Still, life has some possibility left. Perhaps this

is its way of fighting back, that sometimes

something happens better than all the riches

or power in the world. It could be anything,

but very likely you notice it in the instant

when love begins. Anyway, that's often the

case. Anyway, whatever it is, don't be afraid

of its plenty. Joy is not made to be a crumb.[29]

---

[29] Mary Oliver, *Devotions: The Selected Poems of Mary Oliver,* (New York: Penguin Publishing), 61.

A Hymn to Hum:

Come, Thou Long Expected Jesus

1. Come, Thou long-expected Jesus,

Born to set Thy people free;

From our fears and sins release us,

Let us find our rest in Thee.

Israel's Strength and Consolation,

Hope of all the earth Thou art;

Dear Desire of every nation,

Joy of every longing heart.

2. Born Thy people to deliver,

Born a child and yet a King,

Born to reign in us forever,

Now Thy gracious kingdom bring.

By Thine own eternal Spirit

Rule in all our hearts alone;

By Thine all-sufficient merit,

Raise us to Thy glorious throne.[30]

---

[30] Charles Wesley, *Come Thou Long Expected Jesus*, 1747, Source: https://hymnary.org/text/come_thou_long_expected_jesus_born_to, Public Domain.

A Question to Consider

Often we enter this season looking for "happy".

We look for "happy" through orchestrating the perfect holiday party.

We look for "happy" in our favorite holiday movies and treats, we spend a lot of time looking for "happy"...but

<u>Where are you finding joy?</u>

A Place to Pray

Take this space to journal a prayer or two.

_____

_____

_____

_____

_____

_____

_____

_____

_____

_____

_____

_____

_____

_____

_____

The Third Sunday in Advent: Joy Sunday

Do not grieve, for the joy of the Lord is your strength.

Nehemiah 8:10

Pastor and Author Frederick Buechner, once wrote,

> We tend to think that joy is not properly religious, but
> further that it is even the opposite of religion. We
> tend to think that religion is sitting stiff and antiseptic
> and a little bored and that joy is laughter and freedom
> and reaching out our arms to embrace the whole wide
> and preposterous earth which is so beautiful that
> sometimes it nearly breaks our hearts. We need to be
> reminded that at its heart Christianity is joy and that
> laughter and freedom and the reaching out of arms
> are the essence of it.[31]

"We need to be reminded that at its heart Christianity is
joy…" Our faith is joy because our Triune God is joy in
perfection. In the beginning, God joyously creates—God
seems to get lost in the joy of creating—from His heart
bursts forth great plains, deep oceans, rich forests, dry
deserts, colorful birds, scaled fish, enormous beasts, intricate
flowers, and delectable fruit. Throughout all time and space,
God joyously sustains—gladly giving us breath, smilingly
showering our crops with rain, sweetly sheltering us from the
wintery cold. And in the fullness of time, our God joyously
saves. The Eternal Son takes on the full finite reality of
human flesh so that His gift of salvation might be full, whole,
and perfect—this gift of salvation is given because of "the *joy*
set before him" (Heb 12:2, italics added). At its heart,

---

[31] Frederick Buechner, *The Hungering Dark,* 101.

Christianity is joy because our God is joy-full and each time He acts we see joy in action. Indeed, God's joy—His creating, sustaining, and saving—is our strength.

Prayer: *Joyous God, may Your joy be my strength. May I draw my energy for the day from your delightful works. Today I rejoice in You, the Creator, Sustainer, and Redeemer of all things. Amen.*

The Third Monday in Advent

The true light that gives light to everyone, was coming into the world.

John 1:9

At the very end of each Christmas Eve service, the ushers come forward, and I take the flame from the white Christ Candle that sits in the middle of our well-worn Advent candle wreath, and carefully pass it to them. Slowly, the ushers pass the flame row-by-row. The flame is passed from person to person. From father to son. From mother to daughter. From rebellious teen to retired widower. From divorcee to dainty toddler. From devoted churchgoer to reluctant seeker. Eventually, every single person has the Light of Christ and the whole sanctuary is illumined by nothing but His flame. As the sanctuary swells, "Silent night, holy night; Son of God, love's pure light; Radiant beams from Thy holy face; With the dawn of redeeming grace; Jesus Lord, at Thy birth; Jesus Lord, at Thy birth", this verse comes to life.

Jesus is the True Light; in His light, our darkened world lights up like a Christmas tree. In His presence, we are put back together. In His mercy, we find wholeness. Hum, sing, and contemplate these magnificent words:

Come, Thou long-expected Jesus,
Born to set Thy people free;
From our fears and sins release us,
Let us find our rest in Thee.
Israel's Strength and Consolation,
Hope of all the earth Thou art;

Dear Desire of every nation,
Joy of every longing heart.[32]

Good friend, take heart. Jesus, Israel's Strength and
Consolation, the Hope of all the earth, the Dear Desire of
every nation, the Joy of every longing heart, who gives light
to everyone, is coming into the world.

Prayer: *Infinite, Immutable, Inextinguishable Light, prepare my heart
to receive Your flame, that receiving it, I might pass it on in thought,
word, and deed in this dark and hurting world that You so love. Amen.*

---

[32] Charles Wesley, *Come Thou Long Expected Jesus*, 1747, Public Domain.

The Third Tuesday in Advent

He was in the world, and the world was created through him, and yet the world did not recognize him.

John 1:10

One of my favorite stories from the Old Testament involves old Eli the Priest and Samuel, his Priestly Apprentice:

> Now the boy Samuel was ministering to the Lord under Eli. The word of the Lord was rare in those days; visions were not widespread. At that time Eli, whose eyesight had begun to grow dim so that he could not see, was lying down in his room; the lamp of God had not yet gone out, and Samuel was lying down in the temple of the Lord, where the ark of God was.
>
> Then the Lord called, "Samuel! Samuel!" and he ran to Eli and said, "Here I am, for you called me." But he said, "I did not call; lie down again." So he went and lay down. The Lord called again, "Samuel!" Samuel got up and went to Eli and said, "Here I am, for you called me." But he said, "I did not call, my son; lie down again." Now Samuel did not yet know the Lord, and the word of the Lord had not yet been revealed to him. The Lord called Samuel again, a third time. And he got up and went to Eli and said, "Here I am, for you called me." Then Eli perceived that the Lord was calling the boy. Therefore Eli said to Samuel, "Go, lie down, and if he calls you, you shall say, 'Speak, Lord, for your servant is listening.'"

So Samuel went and lay down in his place. Now the Lord came and stood there, calling as before, "Samuel! Samuel!" And Samuel said, "Speak, for your servant is listening" (1 Sam 3:1-10, NRSV).

This story illustrates just how difficult it is to recognize and identify God. Three times young Samuel mistakes God's voice for the voice of his grandfatherly mentor. In Jesus, God enters the created order in all His fullness, but tragically, despite His best and most obvious efforts, the very world He made fails to recognize Him as God. Have you ever failed to recognize Jesus? Might He be trying to reveal Himself to you today through something or someone unexpected?

Prayer: *Living Christ, give me eyes to see You, a heart to embrace You, and a soul to welcome You. May I not miss You in the neighbor I don't particularly like, the fellow church member I don't agree with, and/or the co-worker who makes me feel just a bit uncomfortable. Amen.*

The Third Wednesday in Advent

He came to his own, and his own people did not receive him.

John 1:11

We were all sitting with our sweaty backs up against the padded gym wall, anxiously awaiting our names to be called. It was the last day of freshman basketball try-outs. Today was the day we would learn if we made the team. Basketball was not my first sport, but I was a pretty good shooter and I felt like I had a solid try-out. There wasn't anything else I could have done better. Still, I sat there in my sweat, spaced out, in a trance, reliving every drill, every sprint, and every shot from the last 3 days. Then the words of the coach broke into my reflective daze, "Arthurs. Come on back." I stood up and made my way back to the coach's office. "Have a seat," he said, avoiding my direct gaze. My stomach lurched. "There's no easy way to say this," he began. I winced. "We don't have a spot for you on the team this year."

There's nothing more painful than rejection. Your dream career doesn't pay the bills. Your business plan goes belly up. Your beloved chooses someone else. Every rejection, big or small, slices and stings. Perhaps what is most painful about rejection is the sheer nakedness of it; to risk rejection is to offer something of your unfettered self to another. Vulnerability always risks rejection. Vulnerability is also the pre-requisite for love. Without vulnerability, there's no grounds, capacity, or potential for love. Jesus vulnerably enters the world and risks rejection of the very world he spoke into being because He is Love Incarnate.

The poet, Pastor, and hymn-writer, John Bell once quipped:

> Light looked down and saw the darkness.
>
> 'I will go there', said light
>
> Peace looked down and saw war.
>
> 'I will go there', said peace.
>
> Love looked down and saw hatred.
>
> 'I will go there', said love.
>
> So he,
>
> the Lord of Light,
>
> the Prince of Peace
>
> the King of Love
>
> came down and crept in beside us.[33]

Prayer: *King of Love, help me contemplate and celebrate the audacious vulnerability of Your incarnation. Strengthen me, embolden me, and empower me to risk rejection so that I might love as You love. Amen.*

---

[33] Poem found in: Leonard Sweet and Frank Viola, *Jesus Speaks: Learning to Recognize and Respond to the Lord's Voice* (Nashville: Thomas Nelson, 2016), 88.

The Third Thursday in Advent

But to all who did receive him, he gave them the right to be children of God.

John 1:12a

Max Lucado's children's book: *You Are Special* is all about a Wemmick named Punchinello. Wemmicks are small wooden people, all carved, shaped, and fashioned by the master woodworker named Eli. Each Wemmick is slightly different in his or her own way—some have small noses, some have large noses, some are tan, some are pale, some are tall, some are short. The Wemmicks all live together in a village and every day Wemmicks do the same thing—they paste stars and dots on one another. If a Wemmick is beautiful, can run fast, jump high, or sing well, she is covered in stars! If a Wemmick is dull-looking, has a paint chip, or is particularly clumsy, he is covered in dots. Punchinello was covered in dots. He was older-looking. His paint was chipping. He wasn't fast. He couldn't jump. As each day went by, he acquired more and more dots. The harder he tried for stars, the more foolish he looked, and the more dots he received.

One day, Punchinello was feeling especially dotted and downcast, when he saw a Wemmick named Lucia, who didn't have any stars or dots! Intrigued, Punchinello asked why both stars and dots didn't stick to her. Lucia replied, "It's easy, every day I go see Eli. You should go see him." So, one day Punchinello finally worked up the courage to see Eli. He walked up the hill to his wood shop and reluctantly entered. "Punchinello!" Eli's deep voice boomed, "How good it is to see you!" Punchinello swallowed hard, "You know my name?" "Of course I do!" Eli said, "I made you!

And I think you're pretty special." "Me?! Special!?" Punchinello protested, "Why? I can't run fast. I can't jump high. My paint is peeling. Why do I matter to you?" "You matter to me," Eli said, "because you're mine." As this truth settled over Punchinello, his dots slowly fell to the ground.[34]

The Gospel writer John tells us: "But to all who did receive him, he gave them the right to be children of God." In Christ, you are God's child. You belong to God. No dot or star supplants your deepest and truest identity.

Prayer: *Father God, today I rest in Your kind, gentle, fatherly embrace. I am Yours. Nothing can take that identity away from me. Amen.*

[34] Max Lucado, *You Are Special: Anniversary Pop-Up Edition*, (United Kingdom: Lion Hudson PLC, 2015).

The Third Friday in Advent

The Word became flesh and dwelt among us.

John 1:14a

In his book, *The Signature of Jesus,* Brennan Manning tells the story of Fr. Dominique Voillaume. Dominique Voillaume was a Franciscan Priest in a small open monastery in Saint Remy, France. He was a lean, muscular six feet, two inches, always wearing a navy-blue beret. At age fifty-four he learned that he was dying of inoperable cancer. With the monastery's permission, he moved to a poor neighborhood in Paris and took a job as a night watchman at a factory. Returning home every morning at 8:00 a.m., he would go directly to a little park across the street from where he lived and sit down on a wooden bench. Hanging around the park were marginal people—drifters, winos, "has-beens", dirty old men who ogled the girls passing by. Dominique never criticized, scolded, or reprimanded them. He laughed, told stories, shared his candy, and accepted them just as they were. From living so long in the monastery, he gave off a peace, a serene sense of self-possession, and a hospitality of heart that caused cynical young men and defeated old men to gravitate toward him like bacon and eggs. His simple witness lay in accepting others as they were without questions and allowing them to make themselves at home in his heart. He loved with the heart of Jesus. The Word was enfleshed on his bones.

One morning Dominique failed to appear on his park bench. The men grew concerned. A few hours later, he was found dead on the floor of his flat. Dominique Voillaume was laid to rest in an unadorned pine box in the backyard of the Monastery he lived in for so many years in Saint Remy. Over his grave was a simple cross with the inscription: "Dominique Voillaume, a witness to Jesus Christ". More than seven thousand people gathered from all over Europe to attend his funeral, including the drifters, winos, "has beens", and dirty old men who Dominique sat with all those nights on the park bench.[35]

Eugene Peterson's translation of John 1:14a goes like this: "The Word became flesh and blood and moved into the neighborhood" (John 1:14a MSG). In Jesus, God comes down and takes up residence on our street as Dominique Voillaume took up residence on that Parisian park bench with the unlovely and discarded.

Prayer: *Hospitable and Kind God, You move into my neighborhood despite all within me that is crooked, cracked, and calloused. Come close to me; that I may be transformed by Your hospitable healing presence. Amen.*

---

[35] Brennan, Manning, *The Signature of Jesus,* (Sisters, Or: Multnomah, 2004), 97-99.

The Third Saturday in Advent

We observed his glory, the glory as the one and only Son from the Father, full of grace and truth.

John 1:14b

Jesus is full of grace and full of truth. The Gospel writer John says in Jesus, "there is grace upon grace" (Jn 1:16). In another place in John's Gospel Jesus calls Himself, "the way, *the truth,* and the life" (Jn 14:6, italics added). Jesus is the full embodiment of grace and truth. But there seems to be an inherent tension between grace and truth. Isn't grace unconditional acceptance or unmerited favor? And isn't truth getting to the heart of what's real and embodying what is *truly* good? How can one be full of grace—unconditional acceptance—*and* full of truth—embodying *true* goodness?

There's perhaps no better place to see the dynamic between grace and truth at play than in the practice of parenting. Sara and I are not parents to any biological or adopted children, but we are puppy parents to an overly excited eleven-pound miniature dachshund named Penny. In our puppy parenting, we're still learning to master the dance of grace and truth. Too much grace—not going for walks when Penny doesn't want to walk on a perfectly decent day—and Penny thinks she rules the roost and can do whatever she wants. Too much truth—dragging Penny on the sidewalk for her afternoon walk when it's 100 degrees out, effectively cooking her low-riding hot dog body—and any affection Penny had for us will inevitably wane. When we're all grace, there are no defined limits for right behavior. When we're all truth, suffocating legalistic rigidity leaves no room to breathe.

Jesus is full of grace *and* truth. His grace sets us free; His truth shows us how to freely live. In His grace, there's truth; in His truth, there's grace.

Prayer: *God of Grace and Truth, I rest in Your grace and embrace Your truth. Teach me Your divine dance of grace and truth—help me to be grace-full and truth-full today. Amen.*

WEEK 4
LOVE

Defining Love

Love (ˈləv): *To hold dear; to cherish.*[36]

""

God is love and all who live in love live in God.

St. John[37]

""

Christ is love covered over in human flesh.

Thomas Goodwin[38]

---

[36] Merriam-Webster.com Dictionary, s.v. "love," accessed August 26, 2022, https://www.merriam-webster.com/dictionary/love.

[37] 1 John 4:16, NRSV.

[38] Thomas Goodwin, "The Heart of Christ in Heaven Towards Sinners on Earth," *The Works of Thomas Goodwin, Volume 4* (Grand Rapids, MI: Reformation Heritage, 1862/2006), 4: 116.

Defining Love (cont.)

חֶסֶד (*kheh'-sed*): goodness; kindness[39]; faithful love in action.

ἀγάπη (*ag-ah'-pay*): love; goodwill; benevolence; selflessness.[40]

Because you are precious in my sight

and honored and I **love** *you,*

I give people in return for you,

nations in exchange for your life.

Isaiah 43:4 (NRSV)

There is not greater **love** *than this: that one lay down one's life for one's friends.*

John 15:13 (NRSV)

---

[39] *Strong's Bible Concordance*, s.v. "chesed", accessed August 26, 2022, https://biblehub.com/hebrew/2618.htm

[40] *Strong's Bible Concordance*, s.v. "agape", accessed August 26, 2022, https://biblehub.com/greek/26.htm

A Poem to Ponder

<u>The Cradle</u>

By: Eugene Peterson

For us who have only known approximate fathers

And mothers manqué, this child is a surprise:

A sudden coming true of all we hoped

Might happen. Hoarded hopes fed by prophecies,

Old sermons and song fragments, now cry

Coo and gurgle in the cradle, a babbling

Proto-language which as soon as it gets

A tongue (and we, of course, grow open ears)

Will say the big nouns: joy, glory, peace;

And live the best verbs: love, forgive, save.

Along with the swaddling clothes the words are washed

of every soiling sentiment, scrubbed clean of

All failed promises, then hung in the world's

Backyard dazzling white, billowing gospel.[41]

---

[41] Eugene H Peterson, *Holy Luck: Selected Poems*, (New York: Rosetta Books, 2017), 1.

A Hymn to Hum: Hark! The Herald Angel Sing

1 Hark! The herald angels sing,
"Glory to the newborn King:
peace on earth, and mercy mild,
God and sinners reconciled!"
Joyful, all ye nations, rise,
join the triumph of the skies;
with th'angelic hosts proclaim,
"Christ is born in Bethlehem!"

Refrain:
Hark! The herald angels sing,
"Glory to the newborn King"

2 Christ, by highest heaven adored,
Christ, the everlasting Lord,
late in time behold him come,
offspring of the Virgin's womb:
veiled in flesh the Godhead see;
hail th' incarnate Deity,
pleased with us in flesh to dwell,
Jesus, our Immanuel. Refrain

3 Hail the heaven-born Prince of Peace!
Hail the Sun of Righteousness!
Light and life to all he brings,
risen with healing in his wings.
Mild he lays his glory by,
born that we no more may die,
born to raise us from the earth,
born to give us second birth. Refrain[42]

---

[42] Charles Wesley, *Hark! The Herald Angel Sing*, 1739, Source: https://hymnary.org/text/hark_the_herald_angels_sing_glory_to#Alterer, Public Domain.

A Question to Consider

Have you turned on the Hallmark Channel this Advent?

After a few funny mishaps, the unlikely couple falls "in love", kisses under the mistletoe, and lives happily ever after.

Is this infatuation and passion, love?

Or does the true essence of love look more like God in a manger?

A Place to Pray

Take this space to journal a prayer or two.

_____

_____

_____

_____

_____

_____

_____

_____

_____

_____

_____

_____

_____

_____

_____

_____

The Fourth Sunday in Advent: Love Sunday

Love is patient; love is kind; love is not envious or boastful or arrogant or rude. It does not insist on its own way; it is not irritable; it keeps no record of wrongs; it does not rejoice in wrongdoing but rejoices in the truth. It bears all things, believes all things, hopes all things, and endures all things. Love never fails.

1 Corinthians 13:4-8

If you've ever attended a wedding, chances are, you've heard this beloved passage from Paul's first letter to the church in Corinth. And while this passage reads like top-notch marital advice, it's important to understand that Paul did not write to a wide-eyed, bushy-tailed bride and groom, but rather to a church that was deeply divided.

The situation at the Corinthian Church was a massive mess. Some wealthier members of the church were refusing to celebrate the Lord's Supper with their less affluent brothers and sisters. Some members were babbling in tongues during worship and were boasting that their gift of tongues was far superior than any other measly spiritual gift. The church at Corinth was cliquey, confused, and chaotic. So, Pastor Paul paints a word picture of how the Corinthian Christians should treat one another: lovingly.

An unintended consequence of this beautiful invitation to love is the way in which this passage perfectly describes the person of Jesus. Humor me as I replace the word "love" with "Jesus".

Jesus is patient (He puts up with his faithless and fickle disciples time and time again [Mt 14, Mk 8, Mk 10, etc.]), Jesus is kind (to the woman caught in adultery [Jn 8:1-11], to the paralytic [Mt 9:1-8], to the blind man [Jn 9:1-12], to the woman who was hemorrhaging [Lk 8:42-48], and to so many more, including you and me), Jesus is not envious or boastful or arrogant or rude ("Jesus, who though he was in the form of God, did not regard equality with God as something to be exploited, but emptied himself" [Phil 2:6]), Jesus does not insist on his own way ("Father, not my will, but yours be done" [Mk 14:36]), Jesus is not irritable (how many ill-intentioned questions did Jesus welcome from the Pharisees? [Mt 12, 16, 22, etc.]), Jesus keeps no record of wrongs (Did Jesus hold Peter's denials [3!] against him? [Jn 21]), Jesus does not rejoice in wrongdoing but rejoices in truth (Jesus said to the woman caught in adultery, "Leave your life of sin"[Jn 8:10-11]), Jesus bears all things (The entire weight of humanity's sin [1 Pt 2:24]), trusts all things ("Father, into your hands I commend my spirit" [Lk 23:46]), hopes all things ("Very truly, I tell you, the one who believes in me will also do the works that I do and, will do even greater works than these" [Jn 14:12]), and endures all things ("Nothing in all of creation can separate us from the love of God in Christ Jesus our Lord" [Rom 8:31]). Jesus never fails.

Thomas Goodwin, the great Puritan preacher once wrote, "Christ is love covered over in human flesh."[43] Love looks like God in a manger; Love Incarnate will be with us soon.

Prayer: *Jesus Christ, Love Incarnate, I look upon who You are and am utterly amazed. You are Love itself. In Your love, make me lovely and loving. By Your Spirit, make me into a mirror that reflects Your love in the world. Amen.*

---

[43] Thomas Goodwin, *The Works of Thomas Goodwin, Volume 4*, 114.

The Fourth Monday in Advent

Thus there were fourteen generations in all from Abraham to David, fourteen from David to the exile to Babylon, and fourteen from the exile to the Messiah.

Matthew 1:17

Pastor and author Pete Scazzero, once quipped, "Jesus may be in your heart, but grandpa is in your bones."[44] In other words, your Christian faith does not take away the patterns, habits, predispositions, and genetics you inherited from your family of origin. If you do an in-depth analysis of Jesus' genealogy, you see the train-wreck of a family line that Jesus came from—an attempted murderer, a liar and thief, a pretend prostitute, an adulterer and cold-blooded killer, a serial polygamist, and a failed king—just to name a few in the Son of God's family tree.

Yet, what we see in Jesus' family line is what we see in Jesus' life and ministry: Jesus is not afraid, ashamed, or offended by the worst of human depravity. In fact, the deeper and more emphatic the sin, shame, and brokenness Jesus encounters, the deeper and more emphatic His own heart is drawn out in compassion. I love the way Dane Ortlund puts it in his book, *Gentle and Lowly,*

---

[44] Pete Scazzero, "The 25 Emotionally Healthy Spirituality Truisms," Emotionally Healthy Discipleship, October 25, 2016, https://www.emotionallyhealthy.org/25-ehs-truisms/.

Your regions of deepest shame and regret are not hotels through which divine mercy passes, but homes in which divine mercy abides. It means the things about you that make you cringe most, make him hug hardest. It means his mercy is not calculating and cautious, like ours. It is unrestrained, flood-like, sweeping, magnanimous. It means our haunting shame is not a problem for him, but the very thing he loves most to work with. It means our sins do not cause his love to take a hit. Our sins cause his love to surge forward all the more. It means on that day when we stand before him, quietly, unhurriedly, we will weep with relief, shocked at how impoverished a view of his mercy-rich heart we had.[45]

On this fourth Monday of Advent, do you know how much God loves you, even and especially, when you feel least lovable?

Prayer: *Tender God, in Your infinite gentleness, come close to me. Help me understand that what I'm most ashamed of causes Your love to be poured out most lavishly. Amen.*

---

[45] Dane C Ortlund, *Gentle and Lowly,* (Wheaton, Ill: Crossway Publishing, 2021), 179-180.

The Fourth Tuesday in Advent

In those days a decree went out from Caesar Augustus that all the world should be registered. This was the first registration and was taken while Quirinius was governor of Syria.

Luke 2:1-2

The summer going into 5th grade I was obsessed with the movie, *The Sandlot*. At the time, I had fallen head over heels in love with the game of baseball (a love that has not faded into adulthood). There was something about the dynamic between the neighborhood ball players: Kenny DeNunez, Michael "Squints" Palledorous, Benny "The Jet" Rodriguez, Hamilton "Ham" Porter, and Scotty Smalls that I could not get enough of. I knew all the scenes—the one where Ham explains to Smalls how to make a s'more is my all-time favorite. I memorized all the lines— including the trademark, "You're killin' me, Smalls!" One line, maybe the most iconic line of the whole movie, is spoken by Babe Ruth to Benny "The Jet" Rodriguez in a dream. The Great Bambino appears to "The Jet" in his bedroom, and says to him, "Heroes get remembered, but legends never die."[46]

"Heroes get remembered, but legends never die." Sometimes, though, the tales of legends, in all of their legendary-ness, take on a life of their own. The facts are painted rose-colored. Shortcomings are forgotten. The glorifying details are accentuated; the embarrassing ones are downplayed. Tales of legends are slowly valorized until the legend becomes a sort of timeless demi-god. I'm thinking

---

[46] David Mickey Evans, *The Sandlot*, directed by David Mickey Adams, written by Robert Gunter, (1993; Los Angeles: 20th Century Fox, 2002), DVD.

now of someone like Martin Luther King Jr, who has been made into the legendary demi-god who "defeated" racism through his Civil Rights activism. When a legend becomes idealized in this way, our great temptation is to lift them out of their historical context and enshrine them on a timeless pedestal.

We face a similar temptation with Jesus of Nazareth. We read the Gospels and we're overwhelmed by all the good He did—healing the sick, opening the eyes of the blind, exorcising demons, feeding thousands upon thousands, making friends with outcasts, teaching with wit and humor, and most notably, rising from the dead! Surely the life of Jesus of Nazareth exudes a legendary radiance.

But, we must not forget that Jesus was a real person, in a real place, in real-time. We must not forget, what Markus Bockmuehl calls, the "bloody historical concreteness"[47] of Jesus. He was born right before a census that was decreed by Caesar Augustus. Quirinius was the governor of Syria at the time. It was the first census taken in a good long while.

God doesn't come to us in vague generality; He comes to us in precise specificity.

Prayer: *Bloody Historical Incarnate God, You took on flesh and entered the world as a real person, in real space, and in real-time. You are a God of the specifics—so I lift up all my "specifics" to You. All that particularly hurts, confuses, and tempts, I boldly lay before Your throne of grace. Amen.*

---

[47] Markus Bockmuehl, *Seeing the Word: Studies in Theological Interpretation,* (Grand Rapids: Baker House, 2006), 192.

The Fourth Wednesday in Advent

Joseph also went from the town of Nazareth in Galilee to Judea, to the city of David called Bethlehem, because he was descended from the house and family of David.

Luke 2:4

Inspired by *The Great British Baking Show*, my family has begun a new Christmas tradition—a gingerbread house contest. For the last handful of years, the aunts and uncles have been given a gingerbread house-making kit and the cousins have been given a gingerbread house-making kit. Each team has 30 minutes. At the end of the 30 minutes, we call our neighbors from across the street to come and judge our creations and declare a winner. Since my fingers are chubby and my hands are shaky, I usually serve as the team spy—sneaking off into the other room and reporting back to my fellow siblings and cousins what the aunts and uncles are planning, while Sara and my sister, Annie, take the lead constructing the house, piping on red, green, and white frosting, and peppering it with a rainbow of gumdrops. The cousin team's sweet constructions have been surprisingly impressive—I'm happy to report that we are looking to defend our gingerbread crown this year!

Jesus' father, Joseph, is from Bethlehem. So, Mary and Joseph must head down from Nazareth which is in Galilee—the northern region of Israel, to Bethlehem, which is in Judaea—the southern region of Israel, for the census. In Hebrew, Joseph's hometown, Bethlehem, is a construction of two Hebrew words: *bah-eet*: house and *lech-hem*: bread. Literally, Bethlehem means "house of bread". It's fitting that Jesus, the Bread of Life, the ultimate satiation and satisfaction of our hungering souls, is born in Bethlehem—The House of Bread.

As you decorate your gingerbread houses this year, contemplate the (not so) coincidental significance and beauty of Jesus, the Bread of Life, being born in Bethlehem, the House of Bread.

Prayer: *Bread from Heaven, You say that all who come to You will never be hungry and all who believe in You will never be thirsty (Jn 6:35). I offer my hungering and longing to You. Fill me, satisfy me, feed me with Your heavenly bread. Amen.*

The Fourth Thursday in Advent

Now in that same region there were shepherds living in the fields, keeping watch over their flock by night. Then an angel of the Lord stood before them, and the glory of the Lord shone around them, and they were terrified. But the angel said to them, "Do not be afraid, for see, I am bringing you good news of great joy for all the people: to you is born this day in the city of David a Savior, who is the Messiah, the Lord.

Luke 2:8-11

Is it really the holiday season if you haven't watched *A Charlie Brown Christmas*? One of my favorite scenes is when Charlie Brown brings his measly, naked, sad-excuse-for-a-tree back to the cast of the school Christmas play. He had been charged with getting a tree as a prop for the play, and, as the story goes, he comes back with nothing more than a standing branch. Upon revealing his "tree" to the cast, everyone explodes with laughter (including Snoopy, Charlie Brown's dog). With everyone taken over by heaves of laughter, Charlie Brown, frustrated and ashamed laments to his buddy Linus (the only one who is not laughing at him), "I guess you were right, Linus. I shouldn't have picked this little tree. Everything I do turns into a disaster. I guess I really don't know what Christmas is all about." Then he yells in a loud voice that echoes throughout the empty auditorium, "Isn't there anyone who knows what Christmas is all about?!"

After Charlie Brown's burst of emotion, Linus, with his blanket in his right hand, and his left thumb in his mouth, removes his thumb from his mouth and calmly addresses his friend, "Sure, Charlie Brown. I can tell you what Christmas is all about." Slowly, Linus shuffles to the center of the auditorium stage, his blanket dragging across the floor. "Lights please," he requests. The lights dim, and a spotlight shines on him. Then Linus begins to recite Luke chapter 2 and all the laughing stops; a holy stillness settles on the entire auditorium.

Linus, the master preacher, recites most of Luke chapter 2. But, when he gets to the part where the angels address the shepherds, something curious happens. Up to this point, Linus is preaching with his security blanket in hand, but as the words, "Fear not!" come out of his mouth, his blanket drops (!), and a smile slowly grows on his face as he continues, "For behold, I bring you tidings of great joy. For unto you is born this day the Messiah, the Lord."[48]

Fear not! Jesus is coming. What security blanket are you currently clutching? Can you, like Linus, let it go?

Prayer: *Holy God, open my hands to drop whatever I am holding onto for security instead of You. You have made me for Yourself, and my heart is restless until it rests in You. Amen.*

---

[48] Lee Mendelson and Charles M Schulz, *A Charlie Brown Christmas,* produced by Lee Mendelson, written by Charles M Schulz, directed by Bill Melendez, (1965; Bill Melendez Productions and Lee Mendelson Film Company, California, 2016), DVD.

The Fourth Friday in Advent

And suddenly there was with the angel a multitude of the heavenly host, praising God and saying, "Glory to God in the highest heaven, and on earth peace among those whom he favors!"

Luke 2:14

We, all of us, often go about our days as if the material world around us is all there is. We smell our morning coffee brewing, we taste our sugary Christmas cookies, we see the bare limbed trees that line our streets, we smell the sharp piney-ness of our Christmas wreaths. We're convinced that what we can touch, taste, see, and hear, is all there really is.

Angels play an important role in the Christmas story, but if we're being honest, we don't give much thought to a heavenly realm, to God's throne room, to angels, to any of that. More often than not we write angels off as foolish and silly—the stuff of children's books and fairy tales.

But the angelic chorus singing to the Shepherds on the Judean hillside pokes a gaping hole in our sophisticated frameworks and modern paradigms. This part of the Christmas story shakes us awake to the transcendent. This part of the Christmas story prods us to consider the possibility that heaven is for real. That angels do exist. That forces, principalities, and powers are realities that live and move and have their being just beyond our mundane assumptions.

This part of the Christmas story shows us not only that angels exist, but that they exist for the sole purpose of glorifying and serving God; they are His messengers, His servants, and His choir of constant praise. Do you have room in your worldview for angels? The Christmas story definitely does.

Prayer: *God of angel armies, I am wary to accept forces I cannot see. Yet, I pray that You would send Your angels to protect me. As we approach Christmas, open my heart so that I might join in their chorus of praise, "Glory to God in the highest heaven!" Amen.*

.

Christmas Eve

While they were there, the time came for the baby to be born, and she gave birth to her firstborn, a son. She wrapped him in cloths and placed him in a manger, because there was no guest room available for them in the inn.

Luke 2:6-7

We over-romanticize the manger scene. Our nativity sets are so calm and tranquil, so prim and proper. To start with, the *wild* animals are all on their best behavior. The goats are not bleating mindlessly and endlessly as goats do but are rather quietly contemplating the newborn Jesus like monks in a monastery. The cows are not mooing aimlessly or chomping rhythmically as cows do, but are instead, angled toward and taken aback in still silent wonder by the infant Jesus' glory. Mary and Joseph both wear calm smiles and exude the peace of a still lake on a breezeless summer morning. Then there's Jesus, of course, wearing His serene smile, as if he just finished an hour of relaxing infant yoga. And we can't forget the wisemen, like our favorite wealthy uncles, off to the side with their enormous boxes just in time for Christmas. It all seems just a bit too tidy.

Have you ever witnessed a birth? Have you ever given birth? Have you ever seen a hospital room after a birth? The whole birthing business is nothing, if not, untidy. Giving birth is traumatic. Being born is traumatic. There's a reason why the first thing a baby does upon leaving the womb is wail wildly and uncontrollably and the first thing a mother does after birthing a child is cry tears of joy and relief. The birthing process is the antithesis of romantic and tidy. But it is, nonetheless, the most sacred and most profoundly beautiful reality of the human experience.

Jesus was born. God was birthed. The Eternal Son, begotten of the Father, spent time in utero. His coming caused Mary contractions. He entered the world, naked and helpless, in the same way we all enter the world. God Himself shared in the most sacred and profound reality of the human experience—Jesus was born. And in Jesus being born, God enters the untidy beauty and the traumatic sacredness of our humanity.

Prayer: *Son of God, You fully understand my human experience. Today I rest in the wonder of Christmas—Your absolute solidarity with me. Thank you, Jesus. Amen.*

Christmas Day Reading

This is how the birth of Jesus the Messiah came about: His mother Mary was pledged to be married to Joseph, but before they came together, she was found to be pregnant through the Holy Spirit. Because Joseph her husband was faithful to the law, and yet did not want to expose her to public disgrace, he had in mind to divorce her quietly.

But after he had considered this, an angel of the Lord appeared to him in a dream and said, "Joseph, son of David, do not be afraid to take Mary home as your wife, because what is conceived in her is from the Holy Spirit. She will give birth to a son, and you are to give him the name Jesus, because he will save his people from their sins."

All this took place to fulfill what the Lord had said through the prophet: "The virgin will conceive and give birth to a son, and they will call him "Immanuel" (which means "God with us").

When Joseph woke up, he did what the angel of the Lord had commanded him and took Mary home as his wife. But he did not consummate their marriage until she gave birth to a son. And he gave him the name Jesus.

Matthew 1:18-25

Christmas Day Reflection

Our waiting is complete. Our longing is fulfilled. Jesus Christ is born. The world will never be the same. God has taken on human form and made His dwelling among us. The Word has become flesh and bone and moved into our neighborhood. The miracle of Christmas is captured in a word we've continually come back to throughout the Advent season: Immanuel. God is with us. On Christmas, the infinite God becomes fully finite. On Christmas, God is finally and enitrely with us.

In C.S. Lewis' *The Last Battle*, the last book in the *Chronicles of Narnia* series, Queen Lucy stumbles upon a remarkable stable. The inside of the stable is larger when she enters it than when she is outside of it. Amazed and astonished, she remarks, "In our world, too, a stable once held something inside it that was bigger than our whole world."[49]

God, who is bigger than the whole world, made Himself small, manger sized, infantile. God is with you. God is with

---

[49] C.S. Lewis, *The Chronicles of Narnia Vol VII: The Last Battle*. (N.p.: Enrich Spot Limited, 2016) 119.

us. Contemplate and celebrate this holy mystery! Jesus Christ is born today! Hallelujah! Merry Christmas!

Made in the USA
Monee, IL
20 November 2022

18215065R00056